INTRODUCTION

Exploring the water cycle

ROBBIE RAINDROP and the PLUM - The Water Cycle Illustrated is a nonfiction picturebook for young children. The story explores the experiences of a raindrop from the cloud to the plum. How Robbie got into the cloud and what happens to the raindrop and the plum after they join is left a mystery. It is an opportunity for kids to consider the story further.

I wrote this book with Seattle in mind but the pieces fit many other cities circumstances. The Wastewater Treatment Division of King County Natural Resources and Parks is an inspiration for the story. I thank them for the great and important work they are doing.

Please contact me with any questions or comments you may have.

Thank you very much,

Eric Smiley
PO Box 23183
Seattle WA 98102

robbieraindroppub@gmail.com

Robbie Raindrop fell from a cloud on a cold winter's night.

Robbie landed on the side of a mountain and sat frozen.

BRRRR.

When spring came Robbie melted and rolled down the mountain into a stream.

HEY!

Robbie met a fast moving river at the base of the mountain.

WOAH!!

Then Robbie splashed, played, and went over waterfalls.

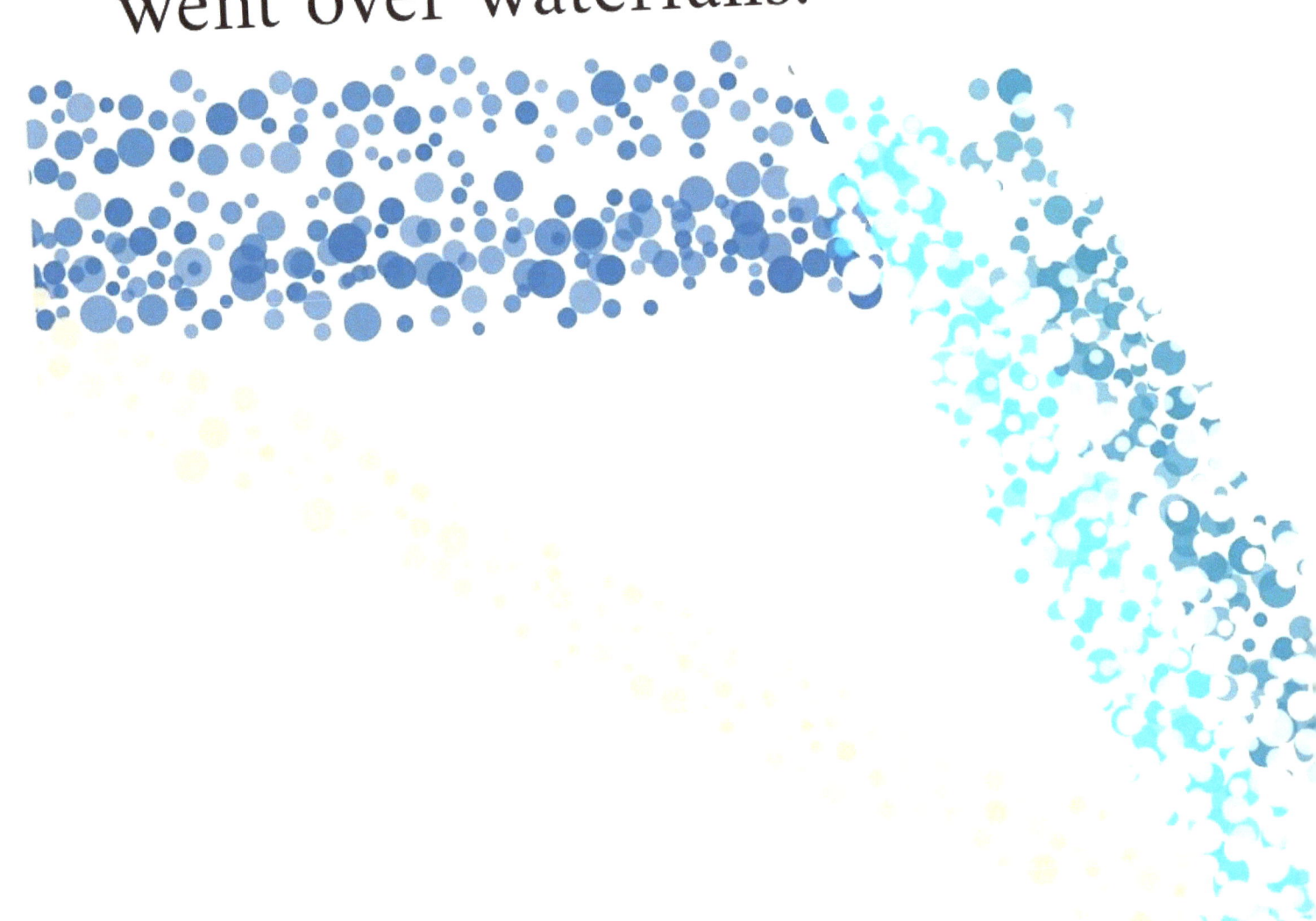

YIPPEE!!!

The Raindrops found their way through canyons.

WOW!

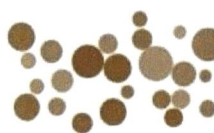

Robbie drifted under a peaceful bridge.

HMM..

Robbie went to work at the dam generating electricity

THIS IS POWER!

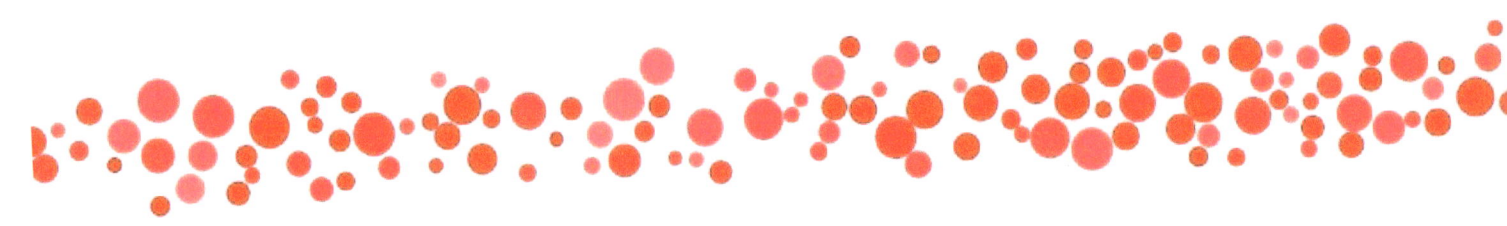

Robbie went past salmon swimming up the river.

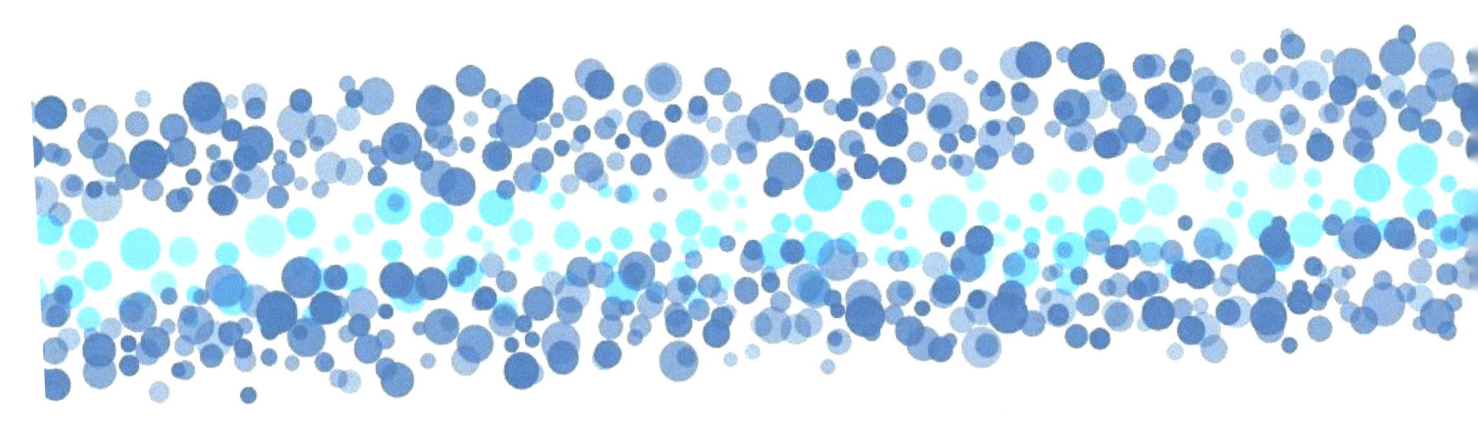

HELLO

And he saw a fisherman trying to catch one.

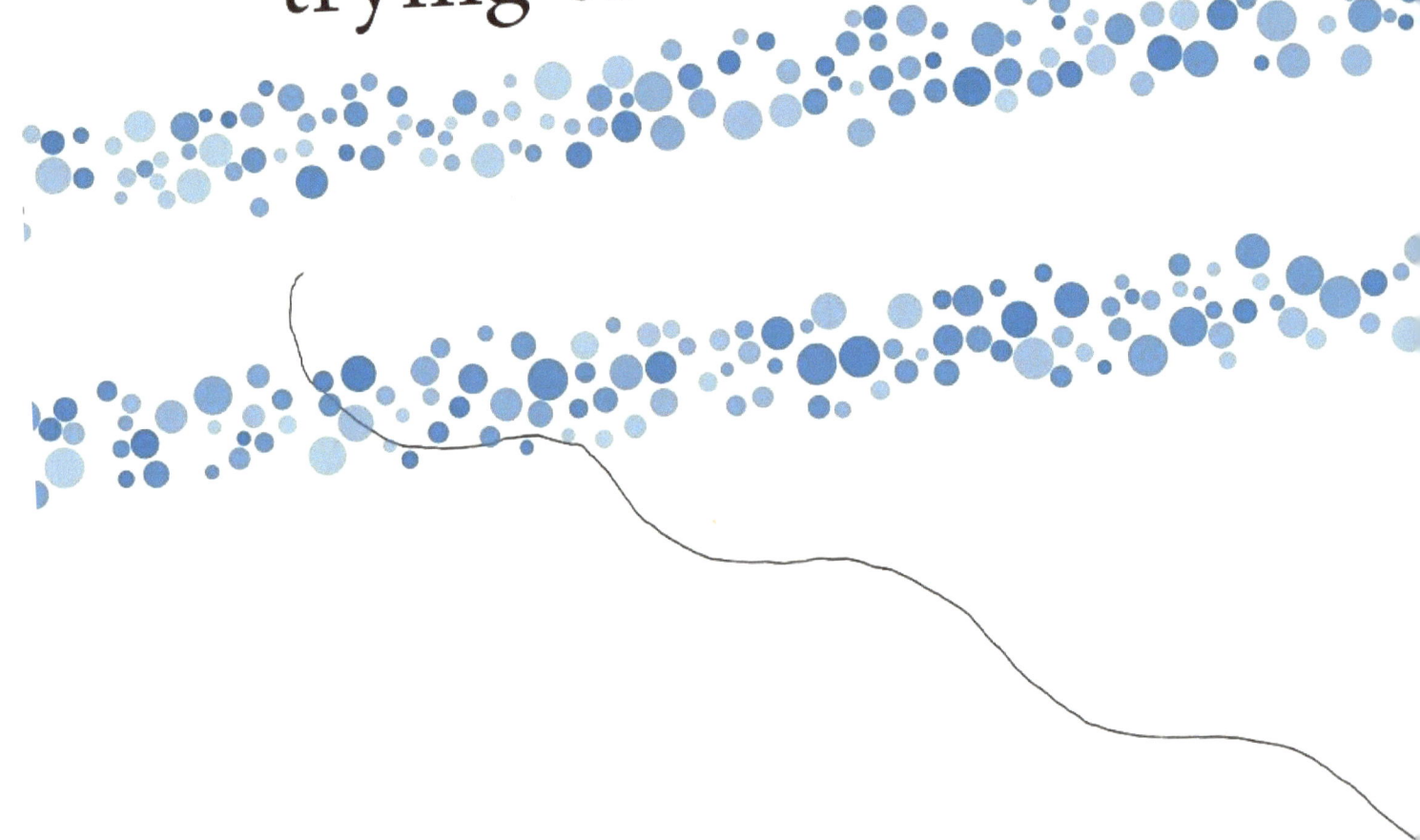

HELLO

Robbie finally arrived at the watershed.

THIS IS THE BEST PLACE IN ALL THE WORLD!

Robbie was put to work in the city water system.

LET'S GO

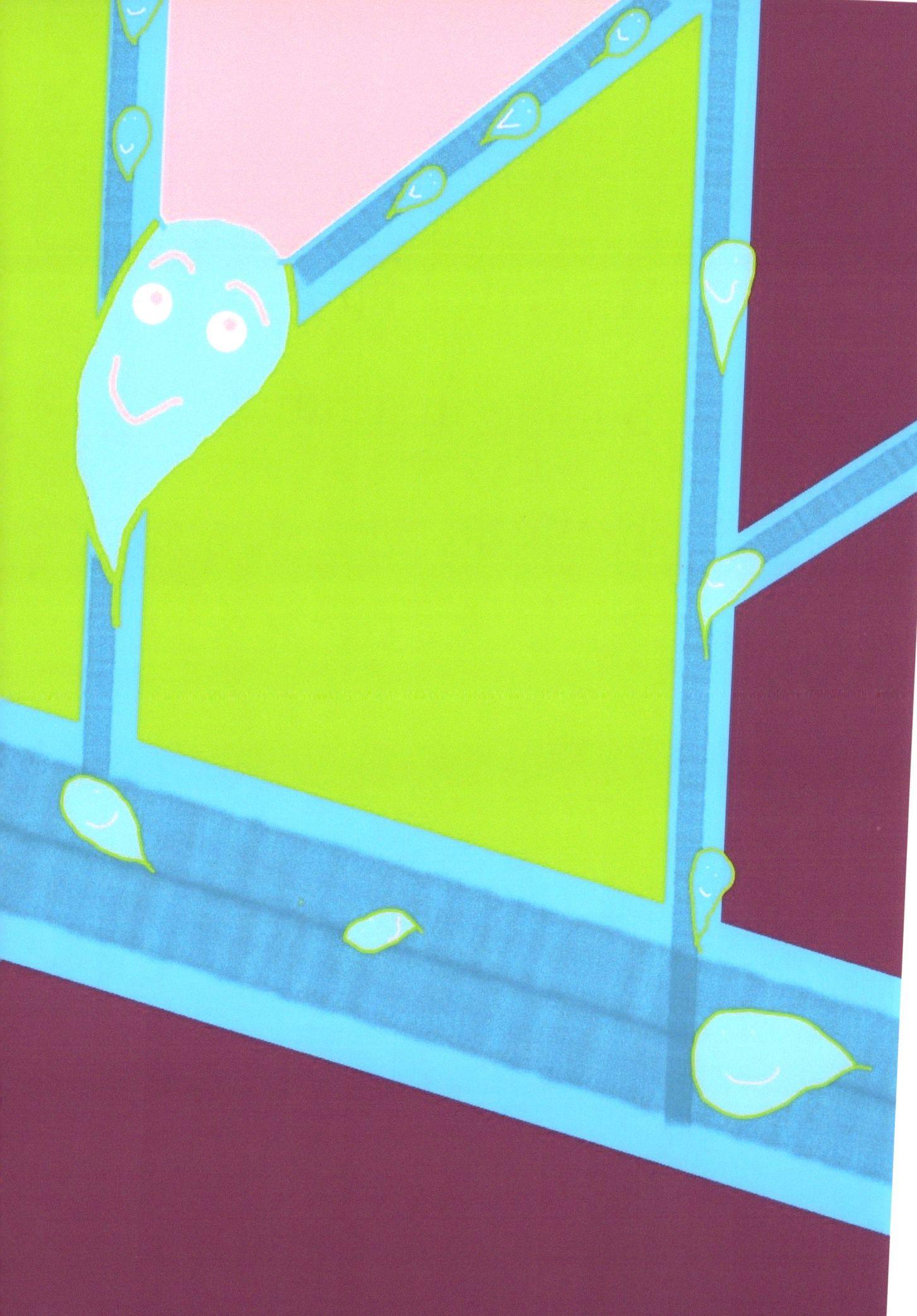

He ended up as a bubble in a family's bathtub.

HEY THERE!!

Then

Robbie went down the drain with the bathwater...

WHAT?

Robbie was in the underground sewer pipes.

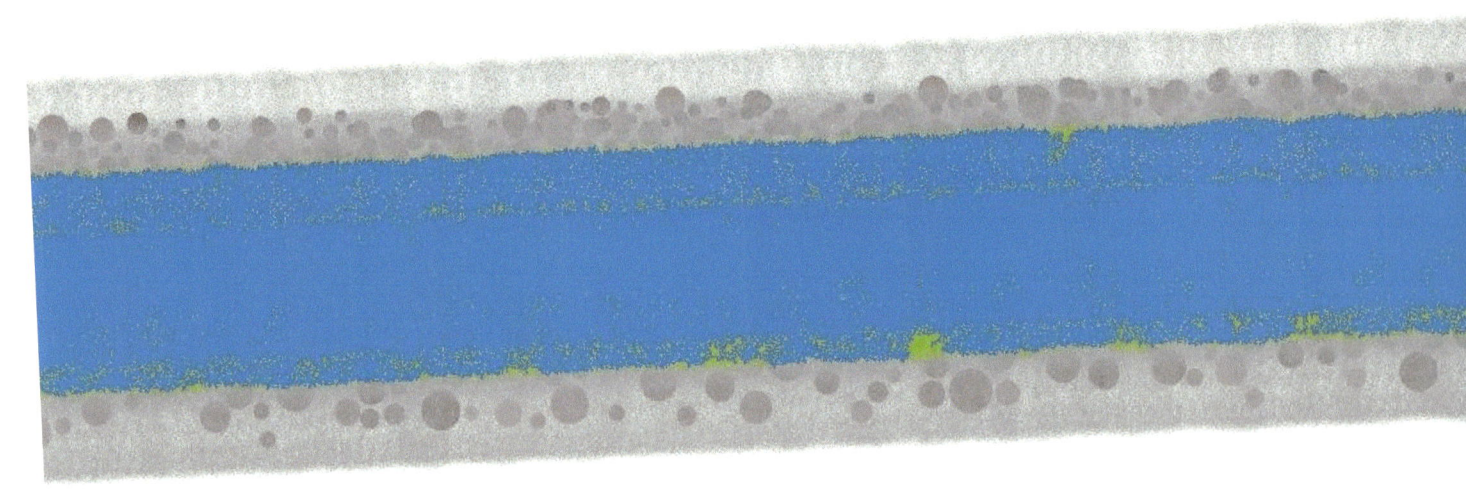

YUCKY

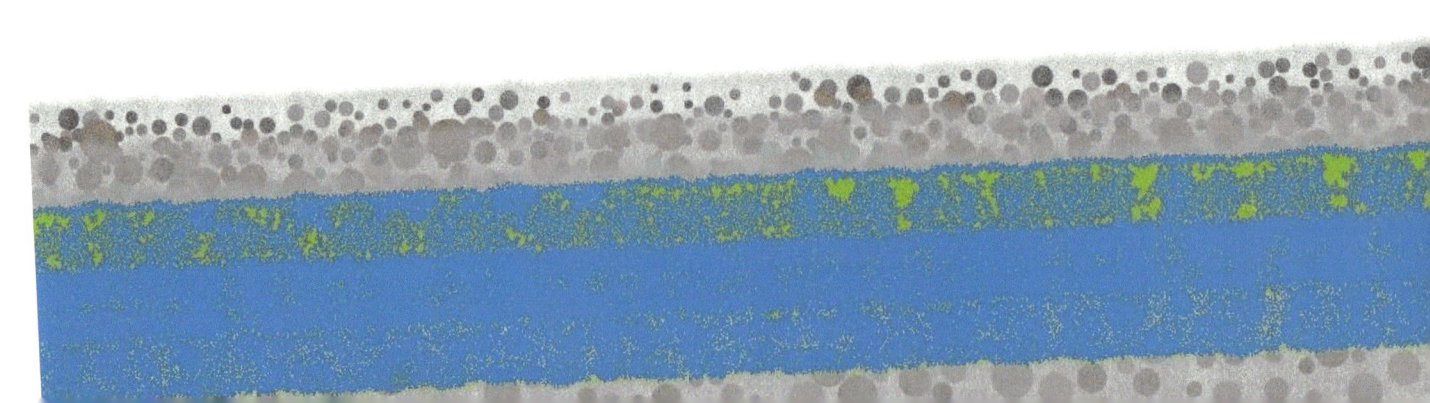

Robbie made it to the Wastewater Treatment Plant.

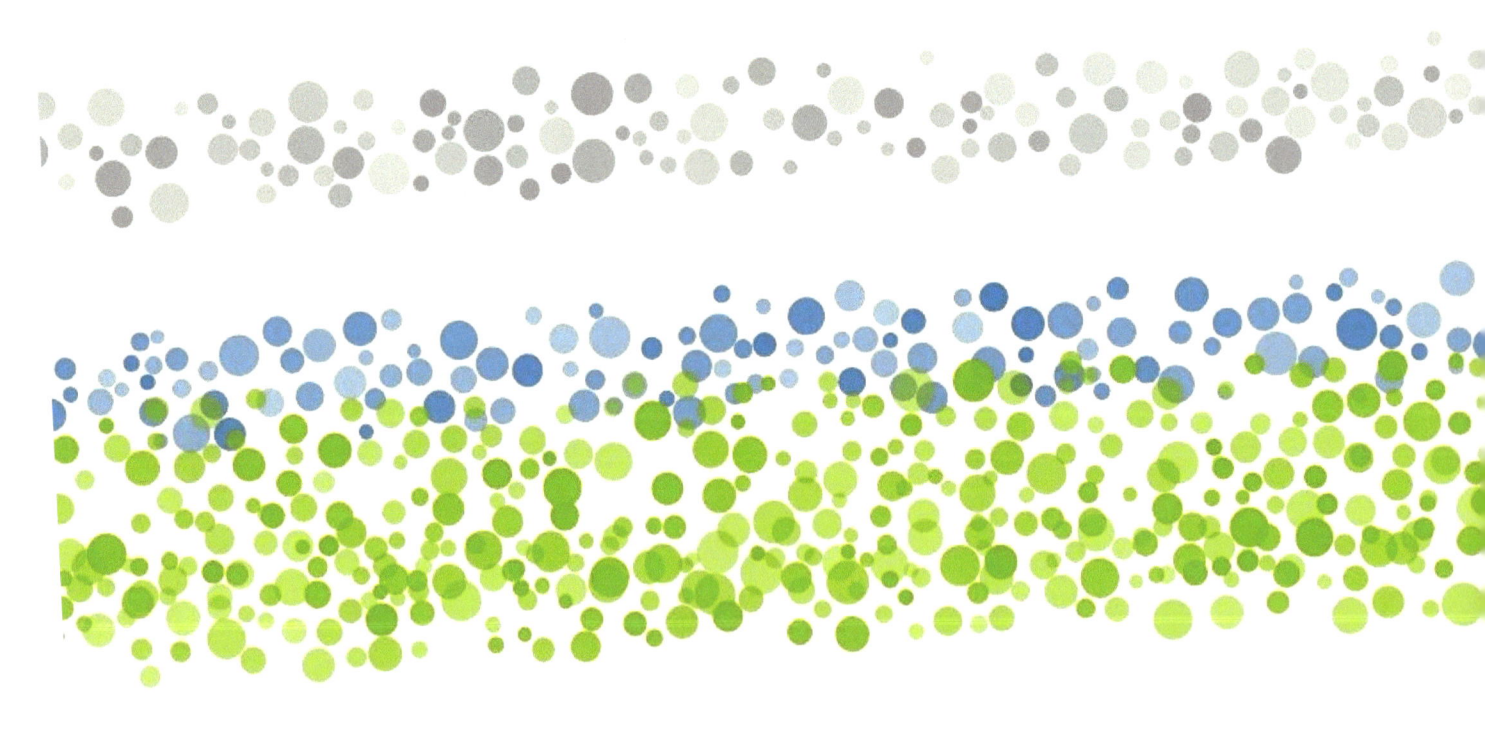

I MADE IT..

A kind woman there treated the water until it was clean and healthy.

THANK YOU SO MUCH!

Robbie was recycled and put to work irrigating a farm.

A FARM!

Robbie went to one of the most beautiful trees on the farm.

NICE

Robbie helped one of the plums on the tree grow big and juicy.

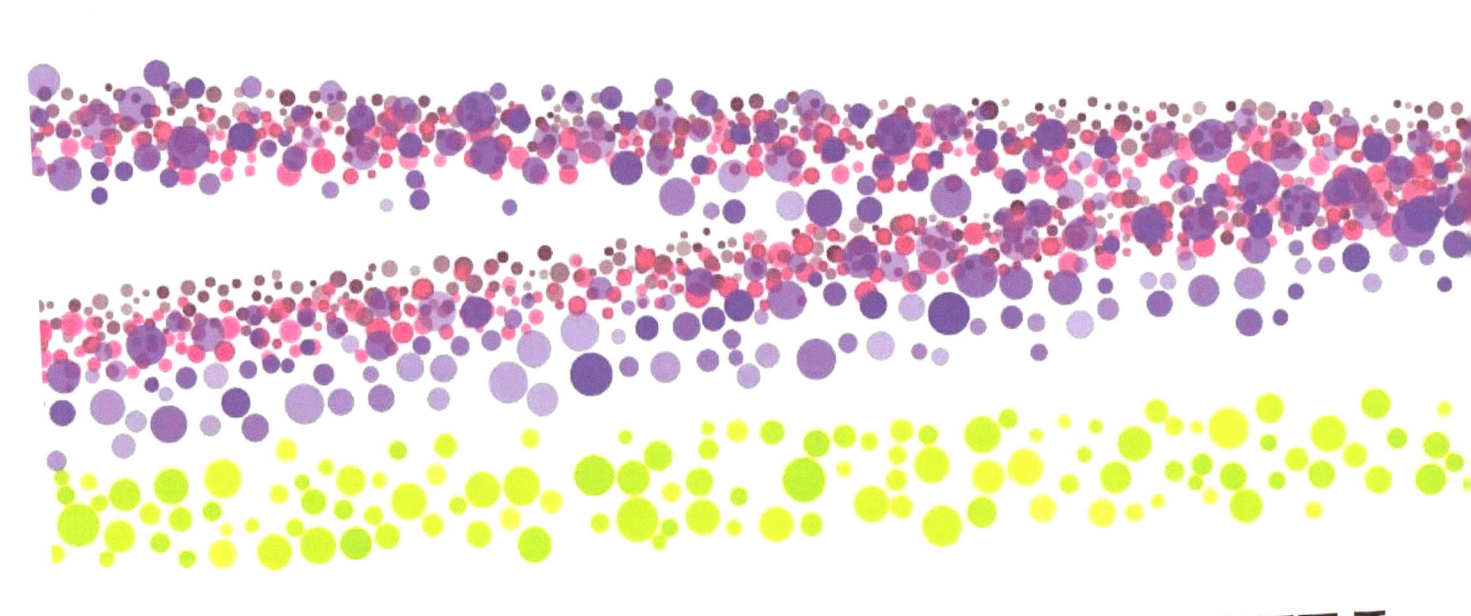

I AM ONE LUCKY RAINDROP!

www.ingramcontent.com/pod-product-compliance
Lightning Source LLC
LaVergne TN
LVHW071027070426
835507LV00002B/59